Dream BIG

American Idol SUPERSTARS

MAR 2 3 2012

Adam Lambert

Chuck Bednar

Mason Crest Publishers

Produced by 21st Century Publishing and Communications, Inc.

MASON CREST PUBLISHERS INC.
370 Reed Road
Broomall, Pennsylvania 19008
(866) MCP-BOOK (toll free)
www.masoncrest.com

Printed in the United States of America.

First Printing

9 8 7 6 5 4 3 2 1

Library of Congress Cataloging-in-Publication Data

Bednar, Chuck, 1976–
    Adam Lambert / Chuck Bednar.
        p. cm. — (Dream big: American idol superstars)
    Includes bibliographical references and index.
    ISBN 978-1-4222-1633-0 (hardback : alk. paper)
    ISBN 978-1-4222-1634-7 (pbk. : alk. paper)
    1. Lambert, Adam, 1982–   —Juvenile literature. 2. Singers—United States—
Biography—Juvenile literature. I. Title.
ML3930.L14B43 2010
782.42164092—dc22
    [B]   2009024495

Publisher's notes:
All quotations in this book come from original sources, and contain the spelling and grammatical inconsistencies of the original text.

The Web sites mentioned in this book were active at the time of publication. The publisher is not responsible for Web sites that have changed their addresses or discontinued operation since the date of publication. The publisher will review and update the Web site addresses each time the book is reprinted.

American Idol ® is a registered trademark of 19 TV Ltd. and FremantleMedia North America, Inc.

CONTENTS

American Idol TIMELINE

October 5, 2001

Pop Idol, a TV reality show created by Simon Fuller, debuts in the United Kingdom and becomes a smash hit.

Fall 2001

Based on the success of *Pop Idol,* and after initially rejecting the concept, FOX Network agrees to buy *American Idol,* a national talent competition and TV reality show.

Spring 2002

Auditions for *American Idol* Season 1 are held in New York City, Los Angeles, Chicago, Dallas, Miami, Atlanta, and Seattle.

January 21, 2003

American Idol Season 2 premieres without Brian Dunkleman, leaving Ryan Seacrest as the sole host.

May 21, 2003

- *American Idol* Season 2 finale airs.
- Ruben Studdard narrowly wins and Clay Aiken is the runner-up.
- Runner-up Clay Aiken goes on to become extremely successful both critically and commercially.

January 19, 2004

American Idol Season 3 premieres.

2001   2002   2003   2004

June 11, 2002

American Idol Season 1 premieres on FOX Network, with Simon Cowell, Paula Abdul, and Randy Jackson as the judges, and Ryan Seacrest and Brian Dunkleman as the co-hosts.

September 4, 2002

- *American Idol* Season 1 finale airs.
- Kelly Clarkson wins and Justin Guarini is the runner-up.
- Kelly Clarkson goes on to become the most successful Idol winner and a superstar in the music industry.

Fall 2002

Auditions for *American Idol* Season 2 are held in New York City, Los Angeles, Miami, Detroit, Nashville, and Austin.

January 27, 2004

William Hung's audition is aired and his humble response to Simon Cowell's scathing criticism make William the most famous American Idol non-qualifier and earn him record deals and a cult-like following.

April 21, 2004

Jennifer Hudson is voted off the show in 7th place, and goes on to win the role of Effie in *Dreamgirls,* for which she wins an Academy Award, a Golden Globe Award, and a Grammy Award.

May 26, 2004

- *American Idol* Season 3 finale airs with 65 million viewers casting their votes.
- Fantasia Barrino is crowned the winner and Diana DeGarmo is the runner-up.
- Fantasia soon becomes the first artist in the history of Billboard to debut at number one with her first single.

May 10, 2006
Chris Daughtry is voted off the show in 4th place, and soon after forms the band, Daughtry, and releases its debut album, which becomes number one on the charts, wins many awards, and finds huge commercial success.

April 26, 2006
Kellie Pickler is voted off the show in 6th place, and soon releases her debut album, which rockets to number one on the Billboard Top Country Album chart.

January 17, 2006
American Idol Season 5 premieres and for the first time airs in high definition.

May 24, 2006
- *American Idol* Season 5 finale airs.
- Taylor Hicks is the winner and Katharine McPhee the runner-up.
- Elliot Yamin, the second runner-up, goes on to release his debut album, which goes gold.

January 16, 2007
American Idol Season 6 premieres.

April 2007
The *American Idol* Songwriting Contest is announced.

January 15, 2008
American Idol Season 7 airs with a four-hour two-day premiere.

April 9, 2008
Idol Gives Back returns for its second year.

May 21, 2008
- *American Idol* Season 7 finale airs.
- David Cook wins with 54.6 million votes and David Archuleta is the runner-up with 42.9 million votes.
- Both Davids go on to tremendous post-Idol success with successful albums and singles.

2005   2006   2007   2008   2009

May 25, 2005
- *American Idol* Season 4 finale airs.
- Carrie Underwood wins and Bo Bice is the runner-up.
- Carrie goes on to become one of the most successful Idol winners, selling millions of albums and winning scores of major awards.

January 18, 2005
- *American Idol* Season 4 premieres.
- Some rules change:
  - The age limit is raised from 24 to 28.
  - The semi-final competition is separated by gender up until the 12 finalists.

April 24–25, 2007
American Idol Gives Back, a charitable campaign to raise money for underprivileged children worldwide, airs, and raises more than $70 million.

May 23, 2007
- *American Idol* Season 6 finale airs.
- Jordin Sparks wins with 74 million votes and Blake Lewis is the runner-up.
- Jordin goes on to join Kelly Clarkson and Carrie Underwood in the ranks of highly successful post-Idol recording artists.

January 13, 2009
American Idol Season 8 premieres adding Kara DioGuardi as a fourth judge.

February 14, 2009
The American Idol Experience, a theme park attraction, officially opens at Disney's Hollywood Studio in Florida.

May 20, 2009
- *American Idol* Season 8 finale airs.
- Kris Allen unexpectedly wins and Adam Lambert is the runner-up.
- Almost 100 million people voted in the season 8 finale.

Adam Lambert waves to the crowd during his homecoming parade in San Diego, California, after making it into the *American Idol* final three in 2009. From the beginning of his *Idol* journey, Adam had charmed TV audiences and impressed them with his vocal talent. For many, he was already a star.

1

A Star's Homecoming

Adam Lambert returned home to a hero's welcome on May 8, 2009. The 26-year-old had captured the hearts, minds, and imaginations of the public with his thrilling, energetic performances on *American Idol*. He had, to no one's surprise, made it to the final three, and as was traditional on the show, returned to his home in San Diego to celebrate.

Adam was unlike anything *Idol* had ever seen before. He was blessed with an incredible voice—powerful, **unrelenting**, and with incredible vocal range. He oozed **charisma** from the very first moment he stepped onto the stage, and often accompanied his performances with a dynamic, theatrical style. Adam's clothing, hairstyle, and appearance further enhanced his artistry, as *Los Angeles Times* fashion critic Booth Moore pointed out:

> **❝I'm obsessed with Lambert's style and his dark, Elvis Presley-like good looks. . . . I can't wait to see what becomes of Lambert's career. With his fashion sense, he has to be the next David Bowie.❞**

Adam arrived at his first destination, the Fox 5 Morning News studios, at 7 A.M. He showed up in style, too—riding in the white *American Idol* stretch limousine and stepping onto a makeshift red carpet while his fans gathered around. He definitely received the star treatment, but there was a good reason for that. After all, in many ways, Adam Lambert already was a star—especially in his own hometown.

Welcome Home, Adam Lambert

First on Adam's agenda for the day was a series of interviews. After exiting the limo, he met with fans and signed a few autographs. He then chatted a bit with Fox 5's Shally Zomorodi, who asked him about the *American Idol* experience. Adam replied,

> **❝I didn't think I would get this far . . . I was like, 'I just want to crack the Top 10 and make some money!' And now I'm like loving it, and I realize that it's bigger than that. It's more important.❞**

He helped out during the weather forecast, and was surprised as his mother, Leila, joined him for an interview. Afterwards, he appeared on 94.1 FM's *Jeff and Jer Showgram* broadcast, as well as *AJ's Playhouse* on Channel 933 FM. During his interview with Jeff and Jer, he was called possibly the greatest pure vocalist in the history of the show. Adam replied that living up to expectations like that was "a lot of pressure," adding,

Adam does a radio interview during his homecoming day celebration. He told his radio host he was feeling the pressure of the competition. But Adam also said he was thrilled to be taken seriously as an artist, something he had worked toward for a long time.

❝I'm just trying to have fun and keep it real. No one gets opportunities like this. I'm very lucky. . . . This is what I've been working for, for a long time. This is the first time that it's really **manifested** itself like this. I've never been on TV. I've never been taken seriously as a recording artist. This is something I've wanted for a really long time. "

Adam Lambert Day

Once he was finished meeting with the media, Adam attended a homecoming parade held in his honor at his alma mater,

Adam greets his fans during his visit to his hometown in 2009. The mayor of San Diego congratulated Adam and proudly announced Adam Lambert Day. The whole town turned out to honor Adam for his outstanding performances throughout the *American Idol* season.

Mt. Carmel High School. The parade started at 10 A.M. and featured cheerleaders and a marching band.

About an hour later, Adam performed for a crowd of 4,000 at Sun Devil Stadium. Despite a subpar sound system and a **makeshift** stage, he wowed those in attendance by performing "Black or White" and "Mad World."

Later, Adam was joined on stage by San Diego mayor Jerry Sanders, who **proclaimed** Friday, May 8, 2009 "Adam Lambert Day" in the city. The mayor added,

> **"I want to congratulate you. All of San Diego is tremendously proud of what you've done, and we're excited for you. We know you will be the next [American] Idol."**

IDOL'S HOMECOMING TRADITION

Throughout the history of *American Idol,* the final three contestants have always been given the opportunity to return to their hometowns. There, they celebrate with their fans, make special guest appearances on radio and television, and even appear at live events or hold impromptu concerts. It is an excellent way to honor them for their accomplishments throughout the season so far, and in 2009, it was Adam's turn.

The homecoming festivities often lead to special moments. In 2004, future champion Fantasia Barrino returned to her hometown of High Point, North Carolina, where she performed and was given the key to the city in what she called one of the biggest events in the city's history. During his homecoming in 2008, seventh season runner-up David Archuleta returned to Salt Lake City and performed before a Utah Jazz basketball game.

Before leaving Mt. Carmel, Adam met with students who were active in the drama and choir groups. He then toured the school's performing arts center. His next stop was the AT&T store, where was presented with a complimentary cell phone.

Adam visits the Marine Corps Air Station at Miramar at the end of his homecoming celebration. He greeted the troops and was touched by the military items he was given. But as he left, Adam knew he had hard work ahead of him when he returned to the finals of *American Idol*.

Ending One Incredible Day

Adam capped off his day with a visit to the Bob Hope Theater at the Marine Corps Air Station at Miramar. While it was open only to members of the armed forces and their families, the event marked the first time an *Idol* homecoming featured a visit to a military facility. Once he arrived at the base, he was greeted by the base's general, and was given several special items, including a military medallion, a commemorative plaque, a Marine Corps T-shirt, and a plush version of the USMC bulldog mascot.

Later, Congressman Brian Bilbray came out and presented Adam with an American flag that had been sent from Washington, D.C., where it had once flown. Adam thanked everyone and told them he was touched and honored by their warm welcome.

He thanked those on hand for serving the country, and was then asked to sing the national anthem. It was an incredible way to finish an incredible day. However, deep down Adam knew there was still work to be done. As he earlier told radio show hosts Jeff and Jer,

> **If I were to win, it would definitely be a validation of everything I have worked for. . . . Getting to be on this platform and being able to entertain this many people all at once . . . this is the ultimate prize. This is what I've wanted for my whole life . . . it will be a crowning achievement.**

Adam had made it to the final three, but to claim that ultimate prize, he still needed to overcome a pair of talented challengers in Kris Allen and Danny Gokey. Despite his status as the front-runner, victory was by no means guaranteed.

Adam put his energy into music at a young age. Even as a child he seemed born to perform. Not content to just sing along with music on the radio, Adam always wanted to sing and act on the stage.

2

Born to Perform

Born in Indianapolis, Indiana, on January 29, 1982, Adam Mitchel Lambert and his now-divorced parents, Eber and Leila, moved to San Diego when Adam was only a year old. He was later joined by a younger brother, Neil. Adam was an energetic, borderline hyperactive child growing up, and he expressed an interest in music from the very beginning.

Adam received his education at Deer Canyon Elementary School, Mesa Verde Middle School, and Mt. Carmel High School. He was influenced by the work of Queen, Michael Jackson, David Bowie, KISS, Madonna, and others. In fact, as his brother Neil

17

would later recall through an online blog, young Adam would frequently sing along to his favorite songs on the radio while also putting his own spin on them. Unlike many kids, however, he wasn't just content to sing along and pretend. He wanted to sing and act for real.

KISS

One of Adam's primary musical influences growing up was KISS, a hard rock band originally formed in 1972. In the beginning, KISS's lineup included lead singer Gene Simmons, guitarist Ace Frehley, rhythm guitar player Paul Stanley, and drummer Peter Criss. The musical group initially gained fame not just because of their incredible sound, but also because of their wild makeup, their outlandish comic-book style outfits, and their dazzling **pyrotechnical** stunts.

While the some of the members have changed (only Simmons and Stanley have remained with the band throughout), and the makeup, costumes, and theatrics have come and gone over the years, KISS has consistently delivered hit after hit, including such classic rock anthems as "Rock and Roll All Nite," "Beth," "Detroit Rock City," and "Lick It Up." The band has sold more than 80 million albums worldwide over the years, and has been awarded 10 platinum records and 24 gold ones for their efforts.

Devoted to Performing

As a child, Adam worked with a private voice coach, and when he was just eight years old, he became involved with the Children's Theater Network (now the Metropolitan Educational Theater) in San Diego. He worked with them for eight years, appearing in *You're a Good Man, Charlie Brown, Joseph and the Amazing Technicolor Dreamcoat, Grease, The Secret Garden*, and *Peter Pan*. Kathie Bretches-Urban, director of the theater, told mtv.com,

"On the stage, he always had great confidence. He was very focused and directed at what he wanted to do and being the best and

excelling. . . . I absolutely believe he was born to perform. He had that talent as a young man, and it just grew and grew as he grew up. **"**

Adam was never into sports, but as Kathie later told the *North County Times*, he worked as hard on his singing as an athlete does training for his or her favorite sport. She praised his parents for giving him a "great foundation," noting that they always "let him be who he was" and "supported him wholeheartedly." Adam himself always loved the challenge of performing different types of music, she recalled.

Adam shows confidence and poise that was unusual in a boy his age. He had a voice coach by the age of eight and was part of a children's theater group for eight years. Adam's stage presence and drive amazed many adults who worked with him.

As he grew older, he began serving as a mentor for the younger members of the group, which, according to Kathie, involved tasks ranging from teaching choreography to simply wiping a few runny

Adam shows off his makeup and costume in a 2004 theater production. Critics began to notice him as a teen, and he received good reviews for his roles in local musicals. His fellow cast members thought he was so good that they urged him to try out for *American Idol*.

noses. Despite his obvious talent, he wasn't always the star of the show. As Kathie points out, sharing the spotlight with others "teaches you humility . . . it's like being part of a team or a family."

Wowing Crowds and Taking Risks

The Children's Theater Network wound up being an incredible launching pad for Adam's performing career. In 2004, Adam landed the role of Joshua in *The Ten Commandments: The Musical*, working alongside veteran actor Val Kilmer. He drew praise for his efforts. *New York Times* theater critic Charles Isherwood called Adam "the most consistent crowd-wower." Later that year, he also debuted as part of *The Zodiac Show*, which according to mtv.com has been described as a "rock-and-roll *Cirque de Soleil*."

Afterwards, he was the **understudy** for the role of Fiyero during the Los Angeles theater production of *Wicked* (a musical that retells the story of *The Wizard of Oz* from the witches' perspective). In fact, it was his fellow cast members from that show who first encouraged him to try out for *American Idol*. Though Adam told John Wilkens of the *San Diego Union-Tribune* that he had never really pictured himself on the show, he decided to give it a shot. After all, while he had been successful, he wasn't completely satisfied as an artist. As Adam told realityworldtv.com,

> **The show tune thing, the musical theater thing, was just kind of the way that I was paying the bills. I mean, we all have to have a job. . . . I [want] to finally sing the kind of music that I like to listen to.**

Tired of, as Wilkens put it, "cruddy apartments [and] cruddier paychecks," Adam left behind his days in the theater, packed up, and headed for the Cow Palace in San Francisco, hopeful that all his hard work and dedication to the art of music would pay off. After all, as Adam told Wilkens, "Life is all about taking risks to get what you want."

American Idol winners from seasons one to seven appear at the American Idol Experience grand opening at Disney World in 2009. Thanks to *Idol*, all of them have gone on to successful music careers. Through the years, the show has been an amazing star-making vehicle and a showcase for young talent.

3

TV's Top Talent Showcase

From its debut in June 2002 through the end of its seventh season, *American Idol* has been seen by hundreds of millions of fans who, by voting for their favorite artist, have made this more than just a show featuring aspiring singers. In truth, *American Idol* has become an interactive viewing experience like no other.

Conceived by British music executive Simon Fuller and originally launched in the U.K., the *Idol* franchise found an American home on Fox thanks to the recommendation of network chairman Rupert Murdoch's daughter. While ABC, CBS, and NBC had passed on the program outright, Fox executives were considering it. However, once Elisabeth Murdoch told her father how entertaining and popular the British version was, Rupert immediately sent down orders to pick it up. It was a brilliant move, as the show has consistently been a ratings leader and has attracted legions of fans.

A Star in the Making

American Idol: The Search for a Superstar premiered on June 11, 2002. The show featured British record executive Simon Cowell, manager and producer Randy Jackson, and singer and choreographer Paula Abdul as judges. Former game show host Ryan Seacrest and comedian Bryan Dunkleman initially shared **emcee** duties, though Bryan left after just one season. After weeding through auditions and sending the most talented competitors through a semifinal round, the show emerged with 10 finalists who competed in a series of weekly theme-night challenges.

After all was said and done, two competitors were left standing: 20-year-old Texas native Kelly Clarkson, and 23-year-old Justin Guarini of Pennsylvania. Both obviously had talent, or they wouldn't have made it as far as they did. However, on August 7, during Big Band night, Kelly showed exactly why she would go on to become the first *American Idol* champion, as she belted out an incredible version of the 1944 song "Stuff Like That There." As *Entertainment Weekly* would later recall,

> **❝Decked out in her black-and-white polka-dot dress and pearls, Kelly . . . broke out a monster range that proved more than equal to the brassy, sassy 'Stuff Like That There,' making the dusty gem sound fresh and modern. And indeed, her ability to raise even the sleepiest numbers . . . to pop relevance has helped Kelly make the transition from TV-show novelty act to formidable chart-topper.❞**

Kelly wasn't the only star to emerge from the 2002 season. The show itself had become such a big hit that it was moved out of the summer months and relocated to the beginning of the year. Also,

Kelly Clarkson, the season one winner, performs during the 2002 *Idol* competition. Not only did Kelly's win made her a star, but *Idol* also became a huge hit. The interactive audience voting was a new twist on the talent show format, and fans across the country loved the new program.

in season two more episodes were ordered, and the number of finalists was increased to an even dozen. In the end, 25-year-old Ruben Studdard from Birmingham, Alabama, won. He edged out 24-year-old Raleigh, North Carolina native Clay Aiken in the finale.

Memorable Musical Moments

From the emergence of a beloved yet tone deaf competitor named William Hung to controversy surrounding the eliminations of talented performers Jennifer Hudson and La Toya London prior to the final three, the third season of *American Idol* seemed to have

Season three winner Fantasia Barrino (left) joins runner-up Diana DeGarmo during the 2004 finale. After seasons two and three, some finalists became bigger stars than the *Idol* winners. Both Clay Aiken (season two) and Jennifer Hudson (season three) went on to release successful albums and receive numerous music awards.

it all. Eventually the finale pitted 19-year-old Fantasia Barrino of North Carolina against 16-year-old Diana DeGarmo of Georgia, with the **uber**-talented Fantasia pulling out the victory.

To anyone who had heard her sing "Summertime" during the season, the outcome was hardly a surprise. It was one of the first truly memorable moments in *Idol* history, and to this day is widely considered one of the best performances ever broadcast on the show. As Ellen A. Kim of msnbc.com writes,

> **"Barrino . . . whose rasp reminded listeners of Aretha Franklin, was starting to lose fans for being all swagger and no softness. Then she sat down . . . and belted "Summertime" from *Porgy and Bess*. The result was so over-whelmingly emotional that Randy thought it was the best performance in *Idol* history."**

JENNIFER HUDSON

Sometimes when it comes to *American Idol,* the winner isn't always the person who goes on to become the biggest star. Case in point: the breakout star of season three, Jennifer Hudson. Jennifer earned much praise from the judges throughout the season—especially for her memorable performance of "Circle of Life" on Elton John night.

Despite her shocking and controversial seventh-place finish, Jennifer's life and career haven't suffered in the least. She won an Oscar and a Golden Globe for her performance in the 2006 film *Dreamgirls*, and her self-titled debut CD won a Grammy for Best R&B Album in 2008. In 2009, she was named the Outstanding New Artist at the NAACP Image Awards.

The fourth season of *American Idol* kicked off on January 18, 2005. Prior to the season, however, the show's producers raised the age limit, which had been 24, to 28. That opened the door for older competitors, including eventual runner-up Bo Bice and fellow finalists Scott Savol, Constantine Maroulis, and Nadia Turner. In the end, however, it was a 21-year-old country music singer, Checotah, Oklahoma's Carrie Underwood, who won the show and went on to win multiple Grammys for her work.

Showcasing Star Power

For the next three seasons, *American Idol* continued to make stars out of ordinary people. Season five, which began airing in January 2006, featured an incredible array of talent, many of whom went on to enjoy tremendous post-show success. Included among them were Chris Daughtry, whose debut album with his band, Daughtry, outsold the combined totals from each of Ruben's and Fantasia's first two CDs. Likewise, finalists Katharine McPhee, Kellie Pickler, Elliott Yamin, and Mandisa each signed record deals and went on to launch successful careers. However, the winner of the fifth season was Birmingham, Alabama, native Taylor Hicks, whose 2006 solo album went platinum and led to a 2009 follow-up, *The Distance*.

Of course, not all of the stars from *American Idol* are created solely because of their musical aptitude. Such was the case during season six, when 17-year-old Federal Way, Washington, native

EVOLUTION OF *IDOL* ROCKERS

During the early years of *American Idol*, "rockers" weren't much of a factor, as pop music pretty much ruled the day. However, in season four, that all changed. The age limit increase in 2005 opened the door for Bo Bice and Constantine Maroulis, collectively known as "The Two Rockers" because of their song choices and their harder-edged performances.

In many ways, this duo of 28-year-olds opened the floodgates for rock 'n' roll performers. In the fifth season, Chris Daughtry's rock stylings were featured on the show, and his fourth-place finish helped him launch a successful post-*Idol* career with his chart-topping band Daughtry. Yet another rule change finally helped a rocker claim the *American Idol* title in 2008, as David Cook took advantage of the addition of instruments to the competition and used his electric guitar to captivate America en route to victory.

"The Two Davids" take center stage at the season seven finale. David Cook, who won the crown, soon had 11 singles on the *Billboard* Top 100. Runner-up David Archuleta was also successful as a result of his career launch on *Idol*, with an immediate hit single.

Sanjaya Malakar emerged as one of show's key figures. The judges were never too complimentary about his talent, but America continued to vote for him. Sanjaya was eliminated on April 18, 2007, and ultimately 17-year-old Glendale, Arizona, native Jordin Sparks emerged as champion.

Starting in season seven, performers were allowed to use instruments for the first time, which greatly benefited guitar player and eventual winner David Cook. Following his May 25, 2008, victory, Cook had a record 11 singles crack the *Billboard* Hot 100. That November he released a self-titled album that wound up going platinum. The runner-up that year, David Archuleta, also enjoyed a great deal of success. His first single, "Crush," debuted at number two on the *Billboard* charts and has sold over 1.5 million copies to date.

From Kelly Clarkson through David Cook and everyone in between, the show had been responsible for launching the careers of several successful artists. *American Idol* was created to introduce fans to new faces in the recording industry, and after seven seasons, it was still a colossal success on that front.

Virtual judges Randy Jackson, Paula Abdul, and Simon Cowell appear on *American Idol Encore 2*, a video game by Konami. *American Idol* has proved it is more than just a TV show. It has been copied in countries worldwide and has created related merchandise, charity events, and an annual songwriter contest.

More than a Cult Following

American Idol will likely go down in history as one of the most popular television shows in history. It had long been at or near the top of the weekly Nielsen ratings, and attracts hundreds of millions of viewers each season. The public had developed an **insatiable** appetite for the show, even as it was about to enter season eight.

It had been often imitated, but never duplicated. It had **spawned** a number of spin-offs and sister shows, including *American Idol Extra, American Juniors, The Next Great American Band*—not to mention additional international versions of the show, which were now broadcast in over 40 countries. Furthermore, *Idol* had grown over the years and had become more than just a talent competition, with the *Idol Gives Back* charity events and the annual songwriter contest. As the show's inventor, Simon Fuller, once told *The Times of London*,

> **"Pure, simple television is not that interesting for me; what's far more interesting is trying to create a cult effect."**

He certainly has done that, and so much more. There have been *American Idol* Barbie Dolls, *American Idol* video games, *American Idol* McDonald's Happy Meal Toys, and countless other merchandising opportunities. Also, the American Idol Experience, an attraction that opened in February 2009 at the Walt Disney World Resort in Florida, allows visitors to audition in front of a panel of judges as well as a live audience. The show had not only created numerous stars, but in many ways, it had become one itself. Now, as the television icon entered its eighth year, the *American Idol* phenomenon was about to meet head-on with Lambertmania.

Adam appears confident during his auditions, but he later said they were the scariest part of the whole *Idol* experience. Early in the competition he impressed the judges with his talent. His unique appearance and vocal style led to his nickname, "Glambert."

Glambert

San Francisco's Cow Palace was one of the locations selected to host auditions for the eighth season of *American Idol*. While fewer aspiring singers showed up to try out here than in most of the other cities, one of them was Adam Lambert, who later called waiting in line to audition the scariest part of the *American Idol* experience.

When Adam, contestant number 1877, finally got his chance to sing in front of the judges, he attempted one of the most difficult songs possible—the Queen classic "Bohemian Rhapsody"—and nailed it. Paula said he was "one of the most diverse singers we've heard," and while Simon complained that his performance was too "theatrical," all four judges ultimately gave him their approval. Adam was on his way to Hollywood. His journey to stardom had officially begun.

Making an Impression

During Hollywood Week, Adam continued to wow the judges. He stood out during a group performance of the song "Some Kind of Wonderful," leading Kara DioGuardi, the new addition to the judge panel in season eight, to call him "an incredible singer." Based on that song, as well as on his solo performances of "What's Up" and "Believe," he easily advanced to the semifinals.

This time, he turned to The Rolling Stones—his mother's favorite rock band—for inspiration. He chose the song "(I Can't Get No) Satisfaction," stating that he loved the song's melody and lyrics. Decked out in a black suit, with his face in a trademark rock-star sneer, he belted out a version which led Paula to say:

> **❝I don't even think I'm watching an *American Idol* competition. I think I'm watching an Adam Lambert concert. . . . You're in a league of your own, and you're leaving some people in the rear view mirror.❞**

Kara praised his vocal range, and Randy called him "one of the most current artists we've ever had on this show." The competition

THE ROLLING STONES

Ranked fourth on *Rolling Stone* magazine's 2004 list of the 100 Greatest Artists of All Time, The Rolling Stones are a legendary British rock band formed in 1962. The group's current lineup consists of lead singer Mick Jagger, guitarist Keith Richards, bassist Ronnie Wood, and drummer Charlie Watts.

The prolific rock band has recorded more than two dozen studio and nine concert albums over their career, selling more than 200 million units worldwide. The Rolling Stones have been going strong for more than 40 years, producing such memorable hits as "Not Fade Away," "Get Off My Cloud," "Paint It, Black," "Ruby Tuesday," and "(I Can't Get No) Satisfaction." In 1989, the group was inducted into the Rock and Roll Hall of Fame.

Adam belts out The Rolling Stones' "(I Can't Get No) Satisfaction" during the Top 36 competition. His all-out performance made a big impression on the judges and led Paula to say she felt as if she were at an Adam Lambert concert instead of a competition.

had only just begun, but Adam was already making a strong impression and emerging as an early favorite.

A League of His Own

America agreed with the judges' overwhelming praise of Adam's semifinal performances, and he was one of 13 artists chosen as finalists. Their first challenge was to select a Michael Jackson song to perform live on national television. Adam chose "Black or White" and once again earned heaps of praise and applause for his take on the song.

Paula complimented his on-stage presence, and the way he combined his musical talent with an **uncanny** fashion sense. She said,

> **"Never in the history of *American Idol*, all seven seasons leading up till now, have we ever . . . seen someone as comfortable [and] seasoned on that stage. . . . You got the whole package, and I believe with all my heart we'll be seeing you running all the way to the end, in the finals."**

Her associates agreed. Simon called Adam's performance "in a totally different league than everything else we've seen and heard tonight." Randy said he believed that Adam could record a CD right now and watch it "sail to the top of the charts," while Kara mentioned that she hoped Michael Jackson was watching.

Emerging as a Star

Following a unique, love-it or hate-it take on the Johnny Cash classic "Ring of Fire" the previous week, Adam returned to form on March 25. The theme was Motown, and each of the *Idol* contenders had the opportunity to work with R&B legend Smokey Robinson. Adam chose one of Smokey's own hits, "Tracks of My Tears," and admitted that performing the song in front of the man who made it famous was nerve wracking.

Adam presents a tender, acoustic version of Smokey Robinson's "Tracks of My Tears" during *Idol*'s Top 10 competition. That night Adam emerged as a star as Smokey gave him a standing ovation and Simon said his performance was the night's best.

During a practice session, Smokey said he was pleased with Adam's unique interpretation of the song, telling the aspiring American Idol:

> **❝Everyone I've ever heard sing it, it sort of like crescendos and goes up, especially when you get to the ending . . . but you just kept it tender, and sweet, and soft, and I've never heard it done like that.❞**

During the performance, Adam sported a vastly different look—wearing a modest gray dress suit with his hair slicked back Elvis-style. He did the song as an acoustic ballad, and it was a huge hit. Adam received a standing ovation and a literal thumbs up from Smokey himself, and Simon called it the night's best performance, adding that Adam had "emerged as a star."

MOTOWN HISTORY

In 1959, a Detroit-area songwriter named Berry Gordy was fresh off his first top-10 hit as a songwriter ("Lonely Teardrops"). He thought the time was right to start his own record company, so he borrowed $800 from family members and established Tamla Records. Tamla eventually turned into Motown Records, and would go on to become an iconic publisher in the world of music.

The fledgling company's first two full albums—*Hi! We're The Miracles* featuring Smokey Robinson and *The Soulful Moods of Marvin Gaye*—came out in June 1961. Later that same year, "Please Mr. Postman" by The Marvellettes became the first Motown song to hit number one on the *Billboard* charts. Over a hundred others would join it in the decades that followed.

Shattering Expectations

With just nine contestants remaining, the next stage began with a visit to the *American Top 40* studios. This time, performers were free to choose any top iTunes download. Adam said he wanted to pick a song that was the complete opposite of his "stripped-down, soft, and subtle" performance the previous week. He selected the 1976 tune "Play That Funky Music" by Wild Cherry, saying that there were "a lot of cool things you can do with the melody," and that he wanted to "change it up" and make it "fresh and original."

He succeeded. Once again, Paula heaped praise upon him:

❝True genius does not fulfill expectations. True genius shatters it. There are artists that

have longevity in this business because of their unique and riveting performances. I'll name a few: Mick Jagger, Steven Tyler, and Adam Lambert. "

Furthermore, Simon called the performance "brave" and "original." Kara added, "every week I cannot wait to . . . see what you're going to do next." Undoubtedly, many *American Idol* fans shared her sentiments. They were in luck, because the best was yet to come.

Adam sings "Play That Funky Music" in a fresh and original performance during Top 9 competition week. He again earned praise from the judges for his unique and energetic style, which contrasted with his subdued song from the week before.

"Mad World" and Mad Viewers

On April 7, Adam needed to choose a song from his birth year, and picked "Mad World" by Tears for Fears. His performance was based on the slower, sadder version of the song recorded by Gary Jules for the film *Donny Darko*. As the song opened, Adam was sitting at center stage, surrounded by an eerie blue light. He hauntingly began spinning the lyrics as the audience watched on in stunned silence. He eventually rose and began taking the song higher, but keeping his movements to a minimum to place the focus solely on the vocals.

Adam poses with other top 8 finalists (from left): Lil Rounds, Anoop Desai, Scott MacIntyre, Allison Iraheta, Danny Gokey, Kris Allen, and Matt Giraud. The competition among the group stayed fierce. Adam stayed out of the bottom three for seven straight weeks and later advanced to the Top 3 with Danny and Kris.

Afterwards, Simon said, "Words aren't necessary, but I'm going to give you a standing ovation." He did so, and was promptly joined by the other three judges as well. It was truly one of the most memorable performances in the show's history—and sadly, many viewers missed it.

That night, the show had run longer than expected, meaning that anyone who digitally recorded the episode would have missed anything that aired beyond its scheduled ending point, which just happened to be Adam's performance of "Mad World." Among those who expressed their outrage afterwards was Joshua Molina of hispanicbusiness.com, who wrote:

> **❝Thanks to the constant gabbing of Paula, Simon, Randy and Kara . . . the show ran over by nearly 10 minutes, leaving devoted Idol viewers stranded without their weekly dose of Adam. . . . You'd think the highly slick, polished and overproduced No. 1 show on television, in its eighth season, would be able to run a one-hour show on time, without cutting off this season's main star?❞**

The following week, producers took steps to speed things along, including having just two judges comment on each finalist's performance. Yet the damage had been done.

"The Real Deal"

The outrage over fans missing Adam's performance of "Mad World," and the immediate response to it, showed exactly how big a star the colorful, flamboyant performer had become. *American Idol* fans needed their weekly dose of "Glambert," as he had become known, and Adam continued to deliver the goods. On April 14, following a group outing at Dodger Stadium, the contestants returned to work and needed to pick a song from a movie, which they would then work on with guest coach Quentin Tarantino.

Adam chose Steppenwolf's "Born To Be Wild" from *Easy Rider* and told the director that he wanted to do something electronic with it. He injected some dance-style elements into the classic rock song, leading an impressed Tarantino to call him "the real deal." Likewise, Paula was impressed with his efforts, telling Adam,

> **"The reason that you're shaking up this whole competition is that you dare to dance in the path of greatness. . . . Fortune rewards the brave, and you're one of the bravest contestants I've ever witnessed."**

During the elimination show, Adam joined his fellow contestants to perform "Maniac" from the movie *Flashdance*. Then the following week, all seven contestants returned because of the use of the judge's save, and each was asked to pick and perform a disco song. Adam selected the song "If I Can't Have You" from *Saturday Night Fever*, calling it a song he could "connect to emotionally." Simon called his vocals "immaculate," and Paula again predicted he would make the finals. Adam advanced easily, finishing outside the bottom three for the seventh straight week.

A Close Call

It was easy for fans to simply sit back and enjoy Adam's performances. However, the following week was a harsh reminder that this was, in fact, a competition, and that Adam needed their votes to win. Season eight of *American Idol* was now down to the final five: Adam, Kris Allen, Matt Giraud, Allison Iraheta, and Danny Gokey.

It was Rat Pack Standards week, meaning that the contestants needed to choose a song made famous by Frank Sinatra, Sammy Davis Jr., or Dean Martin. Adam picked Sammy Davis Jr.'s "Feeling Good". Wearing a bright white suit and tie with a black shirt, Adam descended down a red staircase during the performance. As always, the judges loved what Adam did. Paula called him *American Idol's*

Adam wows the judges with his rendition of Sammy Davis, Jr.'s "Feeing Good" during the Top 5 competition. He had a close call when he ended up in the bottom two for the first time. But Adam survived, and his fans were excited that he would return the next week.

version of Olympic swimming champion Michael Phelps, and Simon said he appreciated Adam's determination and will to win.

The following evening, Adam and the rest of the remaining finalists joined together to perform a medley of classic Rat Pack songs, and all seemed well. However, Adam was in for a surprise—he was one of the two contestants receiving the fewest votes. He was forced to sweat it out for the rest of the hour, knowing that this could well be his final night on national television. Ultimately, though, he survived. Matt, not Adam, was the unfortunate contestant sent home.

THE RAT PACK

The Rat Pack was a term used to refer to a group of entertainers in the 1950s and 1960s. While others, including Humphrey Bogart, were also involved with the group, the individuals most closely associated with The Rat Pack were actor/singers Frank Sinatra, Dean Martin, and Sammy Davis Jr., actor Peter Lawford, and comedian Joey Bishop.

Among the classic songs performed by Frank, Dean, and Sammy are "Baby It's Cold Outside," "Hello Dolly," "Some Enchanted Evening," and "Everybody Loves Somebody." They produced dozens of top hits, collaborated on such movies as *Ocean's Eleven* and *Some Came Running*, and combined to win several Grammys and Academy Awards for their efforts.

Rock Star in the Making

The following week, Adam returned to work with guest mentor Slash during what he called his favorite theme week "by far." He had the chance to do the one song that from the very beginning he desperately wanted to perform on *American Idol*: Led Zeppelin's "Whole Lotta Love." In doing so, he became the first contestant to perform a Zeppelin song on the show, and he did it incredibly well.

Randy said Adam was "a rock star waiting to happen" and Simon added,

Adam seems to be a rock star in the making as he sings Led Zeppelin's "Whole Lotta Love" during Top 4 competition week. He had looked forward to the rock theme and always wanted to present that song, so he was overjoyed that the judges praised his performance.

"This could've been an absolute disaster, taking on one of the best rock songs of all time, but it was actually one of my favorite performances you've ever done. The only problem is that nobody can top that now."

Afterwards, Adam and Alison teamed up to perform "Slow Ride" by Foghat, which again brought down the house, and during the elimination show, all four finalists took the stage with Slash to perform "School's Out." Adam was declared safe during the show and would move on. His duet partner wasn't so lucky, though, as Alison was eliminated, setting up the first all-male final three in *American Idol* history.

Adam appears to be the uncrowned king of the eighth season of *Idol*. A favorite of fans and judges, he had impressed the country with his flamboyant style and clear talent. His music career seemed already launched, but first he had to face his opponents in the finals.

The Uncrowned American Idol

Fans and judges agreed—season eight of *American Idol* belonged to Adam Lambert. Week after week, he had wowed viewers with his style, his attitude, and his vocal talent. Lambertmania had swept the nation, and now the flamboyant rocker was among the final three. Still, the competition was far from over. It was far too early to crown anyone champion.

Win or lose, Adam had already benefited greatly just from being on *American Idol*. The world had seen exactly what he was capable of as an artist. He had amassed a legion of fans, including Dane Cook, Ellen DeGeneres, Slash, Jamie Foxx, and former *Idol* contestants Justin Guarini, Elliott Yamin, and David Archuleta.

Whatever happened, odds were he had a bright future ahead of him in the music business. Of course, as he prepared to face off against Kris Allen and Danny Gokey on May 12, none of that mattered. Adam was in it to win.

A Call to Action

The final three showdown—the 300th episode in *American Idol* history—began with all the final three contestants standing side by side under the spotlight. Each competitor would be singing two songs that night. The first would be picked for them by the judges, while the other would be a song of their own choosing.

Danny would go first in each round, followed by Kris and then Adam. For Adam's first song, Simon picked the U2 hit "One." Paula called it a "superb performance," and while it was a solid effort, it paled in comparison to his next song, "Cryin'" by Aerosmith. For this performance, Adam chose no theatrics. He merely stood in the middle of the stage, took hold of the microphone, and belted out a classic rendition of the tune. All of the judges loved it, especially Paula, who said,

> **If [Aerosmith lead singer] Steven Tyler were the mentor, I don't think he'd have anything to say. You set the bar so high . . . we'll be seeing you next week [at the finale], and many years after that.**

Of course, as Simon pointed out, it was up to America to decide that. He strongly encouraged people to call or text their vote for Adam, saying that he "deserved" to be in the finals "based on talent."

The Drama Builds

The fans answered Simon's challenge in a big way, as the following night Ryan Seacrest announced that more than 88 million votes had been recorded. How many of those were for Adam, though,

Adam seems to embody the title of Aerosmith's "Cryin'" during Top 3 competition week. His classic version of the song was a hit during *Idol*'s 300th episode. Even Simon urged the audience to vote for Adam based on his talent.

and would it be enough to send him into the final round? The answers would have to wait until the end of the broadcast.

While the world waited, they were introduced to Keep a Child Alive ambassador Alicia Keys and a child named Noah from Africa, who performed while trying to raise awareness for the charity. Next, Kris's and Danny's homecoming videos were shown. Later, season six winner Jordin Sparks returned and sang her new hit song, "Battlefield." Then the audience got a peek at

Adam's visit to San Diego the preceding Friday, followed by a live performance by Katy Perry. Then, at long last, it was time to announce the two finalists.

Ryan announced that less than a million votes separated the top two. Kris was the first finalist named, leaving Adam and Danny to sweat it out a little longer. Adam had been here before, during Rat Pack week, but he survived the cut. Would he be able to do so again, or was his *American Idol* journey about to end? As Adam stood next to Danny, his arm draped over him, Ryan teased the drama before announcing, "The person competing with Kris Allen in the finale next week is . . . Adam Lambert."

Adam soulfully performs Sam Cooke's "A Change Is Gonna Come" during his final competition with Kris Allen. Although Adam seemed to be the front-runner in the battle between the glam rocker and the acoustic performer, he knew anything could happen when audiences finally cast their votes.

An emotional Adam immediately covered his face with his hands, clearly thankful that the ride was not over yet. He would again have a chance to shine on television's biggest stage.

DANNY GOKEY

Daniel Jay Gokey, the third-place finisher during season eight of *American Idol*, was born on April 24, 1980, in Milwaukee, Wisconsin. Daniel served as the worship director at Faith Builders International Ministries for several years. He was married in 2004, but four weeks before his auditions, his wife passed away.

His wife was a tremendous fan of *American Idol*, so Danny decided to audition for the show in her honor. His trademark song for the year was "You Are So Beautiful" by Joe Cocker. He performed the song three times, including following his elimination from the show. Since then, he has signed a record contract with RCA and plans to record an R&B CD in the summer of 2009. He also runs a charitable foundation in memory of his wife.

Adam vs. Kris

It all came down to this. On May 19, Adam and Kris would square off in what Paula would call "one of the most compelling" finale showdowns in *American Idol* history. It was teased as glam rock vs. acoustic rock, the guy next door against the "guy-liner." All season long, Adam had been one of the favorites, both in the eyes of the judges as well as in the hearts and minds of the television viewing audience. Meanwhile, Kris had been dubbed "the dark horse" and the "underdog."

Yet, when it came to *American Idol*, anything could happen. During the program, each man would have an opportunity to perform three songs. The first would be a reprise of their favorite performance from earlier in the season. The second would be a song selected for them by the show's creator, Simon Fuller. The third and final song would be the winner's single, a song co-written by Kara entitled "No Boundaries."

Adam was up first. He chose "Mad World" from Top 8 week, and delivered it wearing a long, black trench coat with the lights dimmed and a dry ice fog enveloping him. The judges liked it, though Simon thought Adam went overboard with the theatrics. Kris, on the other hand, performed his favorite, "Ain't No Sunshine," and won praise from the judges. Simon even went so far as to declare Kris the winner of the first round.

Adam's Comeback

Adam may have been down, but he definitely was not out. For his next performance, he sang Sam Cooke's "A Change Is Gonna Come." He toned it down for this one, donning a silver suit and simply singing in front of the mike. It was a soulful performance, and afterwards, Simon said he was "100% back in the game." Paula added,

> **"I'm in awe of your talent, and whatever happens with this *Idol* journey, I know with every fiber of my being that you're going to be iconic."**

Kris, too, garnered praise for his second song, Marvin Gaye's "What's Going On," and after two rounds it was becoming clear that both of these talented singers had brought their A-game. Adam's final performance of the night was "No Boundaries," and while Randy said it "wasn't one of my favorite Adam performances," Simon reflected on the San Diego native's complete body of work on *American Idol*, saying,

> **"Over the entire season, you have been one of the best, most original contestants we've ever had on the show . . . the whole idea of doing a show like this is that you hope that you can find a worldwide star. I genuinely believe we have found that with you."**

Shining One Last Time

Simon was right. Win, lose, or draw, Adam Lambert was going to be a major star, and he proved it again during the finale. He had the opportunity to perform alongside two of his greatest musical influences, doing a medley of songs with KISS, then joining Kris and Queen's Brian May and Roger Taylor to perform "We Are the Champions." After much anticipation and live performances from the likes of Cyndi Lauper, Keith Urban, and Rod Stewart, it was finally time to announce the winner.

Adam has a final chance to shine as he performs with KISS during the season eight grand finale. That night he couldn't believe he got to sing with both KISS and Queen, bands who had been important musical influences on him as a teen.

As Kris and Adam stood alone on stage, Simon told them they should both be proud of what they'd accomplished, and that the future was theirs. Then Ryan Seacrest announced, "The winner of *American Idol* 2009 is . . . Kris Allen!" In a stunning upset, the dark horse had dethroned the uncrowned champion, and no one seemed more surprised about it than Kris himself.

KRIS ALLEN

Born in Jacksonville, Arkansas, on June 21, 1985, Kristopher Neil Allen was a church worship leader prior to auditioning for *American Idol*. He barely received any screen time during the early shows, and it wasn't until his performance of "To Make You Feel My Love" during Grand Ole Opry week that the judges even started taking notice.

During the show, Kris was Adam's roommate, and the two became close friends, even as they competed against each other.

Following his *American Idol* victory, Kris has been on a whirlwind media tour, and on June 7, 2009, he performed the national anthem prior to game two of the NBA Finals.

Kris also has signed a recording contract with Jive Records and is expected to release his first album on the label in Fall 2009.

Adam was incredibly gracious in defeat, congratulating the winner and celebrating along with the man who had been his roommate and had become a close friend during the season. As he later told AOL Television,

> **"I couldn't be happier for Kris. He's a good friend of mine. I think he's immensely talented. . . . I know it sounds really cliché, but I really feel like I won by getting to the final . . . to me, it's not about the title of *American Idol*. It was the experience. I made music, and I got to do a different performance every week, and I was**

Adam hugs Kris Allen after Kris was crowned the winner of the eighth season of *Idol*. During the season Adam and Kris had been roommates and friends, and Adam offered Kris his sincere congratulations. Adam also said that even without winning, he had greatly benefited from his time on the show.

able to use *American Idol* as a platform to get myself out there, and now I have a career. So there's no need to dwell on the negative. **"**

The Beginning, Not the End

Adam Lambert's story doesn't end with the *American Idol* finale. In fact, it is just beginning. Thanks to his time on the show, Adam has amassed a legion of fans, and has proven that he can perform just about any and every type of music out there.

Adam looks ahead to the beginning of his life after *Idol*. He has already signed a record deal and is eager to offer audiences a variety of his song styles. No matter in which direction he heads, his future in the music industry seems assured, and his loyal fans couldn't be happier.

CLAY AIKEN

Clay Aiken, the *American Idol* season two runner-up, can be a great source of inspiration to Adam, as he has gone on to enjoy a more successful career than that season's champion, Ruben Studdard. The now 30-year-old North Carolina native released his first CD, *Measure of a Man*, in 2003. It debuted at number one and went on to become certified double-platinum by the Recording Industry Association of America (RIAA).

In all, Clay has released four studio albums, which have sold more than six million copies worldwide. He has won American Music, American Christian Music, and Billboard awards for his work. Clay has also been active in charity work and runs his own foundation to help combat autism. Professionally, Clay recently ended a run playing Sir Robin in the Broadway musical *Monty Python's Spamalot*.

To no one's surprise, in June 2009 he signed a record deal with 19 Entertainment and RCA. Adam is currently working on a CD that is due out in the fall of 2009. When asked what kind of material he planned to record, he told AOL Television,

> **❝We're kind of at the drawing board right now trying to figure that out . . . obviously we want the album to have a cohesive sound but I think it can be a collection of different styles with me at the center.❞**

He has also announced his desire to work with Slash, one of his *American Idol* mentors, and Queen is reportedly interested in hiring him on as the band's new lead singer. Despite his runner-up status on the show, Adam Lambert clearly has a bright future ahead of him, and there is little doubt that he will someday be considered one of the true musical superstars.

1982 Adam Mitchel Lambert is born in Indianapolis, Indiana.

1983 Adam and his parents, Eber and Leila, move to San Diego, California.

1990 Around this time, Adam becomes active in the Children's Theater Network.

2002 *American Idol* debuts on June 11.

2004 Adam lands the role of Joshua in *The Ten Commandments: The Musical.*

He also starts performing as part of *The Zodiac Show* during this time.

2008 On the recommendation of co-workers, Adam attends *American Idol* auditions in San Francisco, California. He earns a golden ticket to Hollywood.

2009 During his first appearance as a finalist, Adam sings Michael Jackson's "Black or White." Judge Paula Abdul predicts he will make it to the finals.

Two weeks later, Adam's rendition of "The Tracks of My Tears" earns him a standing ovation from the song's original performer, Motown legend Smokey Robinson.

On April 7, Adam did the song "Mad World," which earns a standing ovation from Simon and the rest of the judges. Unfortunately, the show ran long, so viewers digitally recording the episode miss his performance.

Adam works with guest mentor Quentin Tarantino the following week, and the director calls Adam "the real deal" after working with him on "Born to be Wild."

During Rat Pack week, Adam finishes in the bottom three for the first time.

On May 5, he becomes the first *American Idol* contestant to ever perform a Led Zeppelin song ("Whole Lotta Love") on the show.

The following week, Adam performs U2's "One" and Aerosmith's "Cryin'" to advance to the finale, where he faces Kris Allen.

During the two-part finale, Adam has the opportunity to perform songs by some of his favorite artists, including Queen and KISS. However, he finishes as the season eight runner-up as Kris wins *American Idol.*

In June, Adam signs a record deal with 19 Entertainment and RCA.

Stage Credits

1992   Linus, *You're a Good Man, Charlie Brown*

2004   Joshua, *The Ten Commandments: The Musical*

2005   Ensemble/Fiyero understudy, *Wicked*

2007   Ensemble/Fiyero understudy, *Wicked*

Singles

2009   "No Boundaries"

"Mad World" (digital downloads only)

"A Change is Gonna Come" (digital downloads only)

"One" (digital downloads only)

"Cryin'" (digital downloads only)

"Slow Ride" with Allison Iraheta (digital downloads only)

"The Tracks of My Tears" (digital downloads only)

"Feeling Good" (digital downloads only)

Awards

2009   Honored with "Adam Lambert Day" in San Diego on May 8.

Runner-Up, *American Idol* Season Eight on May 20.

aspiring—Having great ambition and working to achieve a certain goal.

charisma—Charm, or the ability to attract, influence, and inspire individuals.

emcee—A host or master of ceremonies.

insatiable—Unable to be satisfied; constantly wanting more and more.

makeshift—Temporary, often cheaply made or quickly built.

manifested—Shown, displayed, or revealed.

proclaimed—Announced, usually officially and in front of a crowd.

pyrotechnical—Relating to fireworks or similar explosive devices.

spawned—Created or led to.

uber—A German word that means "super" when used in English.

uncanny—Surpassing what is normal; extraordinary.

understudy—A performer who learns another actor's role so that he/she can take that actor's place if necessary.

unrelenting—Filled with force; not lessening in intensity or effort.

Books

Canfield, Jack, et. al. *Chicken Soup for the American Idol Soul.* Deerfield Beach, Florida: Heath Communications, 2007.

Cowell, Simon. *I Don't Mean to be Rude, But . . . : The Truth About Fame, Fortune, and My Life in Music.* London: Ebury Press, 2004.

Jackson, Randy with K.C. Baker. *What's Up Dawg? How To Become a Superstar in the Music Business.* New York: Hyperion, 2004.

Walsh, Marissa. *American Idol: The Search for a Superstar—The Official Book.* New York: Bantam Books, 2002.

Whiting, Jim. *Modern Role Models: American Idol Judges.* Broomall, Pennsylvania: Mason Crest Publishers, 2008.

Web Sites

http://www.adamofficial.com/

The official Web site of the 2009 *American Idol* runner-up. Adam's homepage includes videos, photos, download links for his songs, a calendar of his upcoming appearances, an email newsletter, and more.

http://adam-lambert.org

A fan-created Web site dubbed "The Official Unofficial" Adam Lambert fan site, this contains up-to-date breaking news on the singer's career, an online forum, and videos from nearly all of his *American Idol* performances (complete with pre-performance notes from Adam and judges' comments).

http://www.americanidol.com/

This is the official Web site of the hit Fox television series, which featured Adam during the eighth season in 2009. It includes tons of content, including information on Adam, videos from his performances from the show—not to mention bios and news about past competitors, the show's judges, host Ryan Seacrest, and more.

page

ABOUT THE AUTHOR

Chuck Bednar is an author and freelance writer from Ohio. He has been writing professionally since 1997 and has written more than 1,500 published nonfiction articles. Furthermore, Bednar is the author of eight books, including the *Tony Parker* and *Tim Duncan* entries in Mason Crest's MODERN ROLE MODELS series, as well as SUPERSTARS OF PRO FOOTBALL: *Tony Romo*. He is currently employed by Bright Hub (www.brighthub.com) as the Managing Editor for their Nintendo Wii Web site.